Dear Family,

What's the best way to help your child love reading?

Find good books like this one to share—and read together!

Here are some tips.

- **Take a "picture walk."** Look at all the pictures before you read. Talk about what you see.

- **Take turns.** Read to your child. Ham it up! Use different voices for different characters, and read with feeling! Then listen as your child reads to you, or explains the story in his or her own words.

- **Point out words as you read.** Help your child notice how letters and sounds go together. Point out unusual or difficult words that your child might not know. Talk about those words and what they mean.

- **Ask questions.** Stop to ask questions as you read. For example: "What do you think will happen next?" "How would you feel if that happened to you?"

- **Read every day.** Good stories are worth reading more than once! Read signs, labels, and even cereal boxes with your child. Visit the library to take out more books. And look for other JUST FOR YOU! BOOKS you and your child can share!

The Editors

For my husband, Alton—my favorite barber.

—JGF

To my Uncle Ed, who got me thinking of art
as a way of life and as a career.

—JH

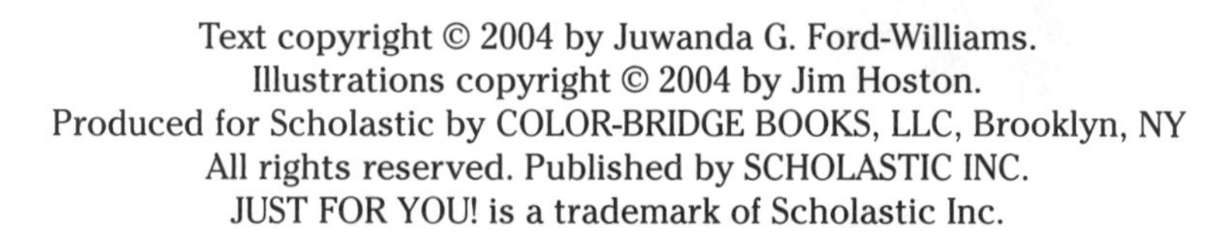

Produced for Scholastic by COLOR-BRIDGE BOOKS, LLC, Brooklyn, NY

Library of Congress Cataloging-in-Publication Data

Ford, Juwanda G.
Shop talk / by Juwanda G. Ford; illustrated by Jim Hoston.
p. cm.—(Just for you! Level 3)
Summary: A boy describes his fun visit to the barbershop, including who he sees there, how they interact, and how the conversation is "different from talking anywhere else."
ISBN 0-439-56873-0
[1. Conversation—Fiction. 2. Hair—Fiction. 3. Barbershops—Fiction. 4. Interpersonal relations—Fiction. 5. African Americans—Fiction.]
I. Hoston, Jim, ill. II. Title. III. Series.
PZ7.F75326Sh 2004
[E]—dc22 2004004771

10 9 8 7 6 5 08
Printed in the U.S.A. 23 • First Scholastic Printing, April 2004

Shop Talk

by Juwanda G. Ford
Illustrated by Jim Hoston

JUST FOR YOU!™
Level 3

In my neighborhood, my favorite place is the barbershop. We call it The Shop. There are always lots of guys inside. Some read while they wait for haircuts. Others come in just to hang out and talk.

Talking in the barbershop is different from talking anywhere else. If you just say, “Yo!” everyone knows exactly what you mean. You can even yell and shout.

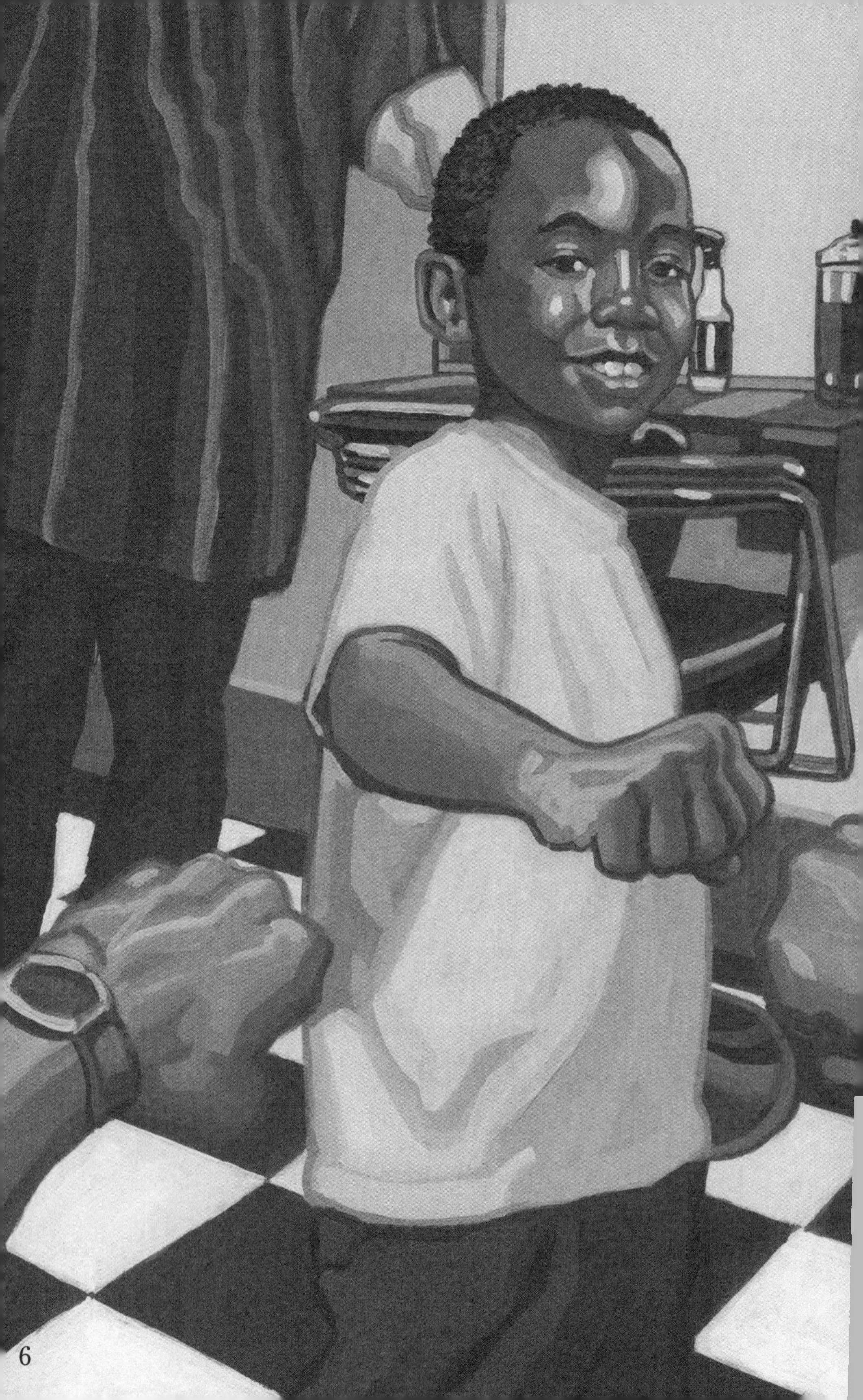

In The Shop no one treats me like a kid. I'm just one of the guys. When I walk in on Saturday morning, all the barbers give me a shout out. That's how we say hello.

"What's going on, Solomon?"

"Hey, Shorty!"

"What's up?"

"Nothing much," I say. I walk around The Shop and bump fists with all the guys. That's the way we shake hands in The Shop.

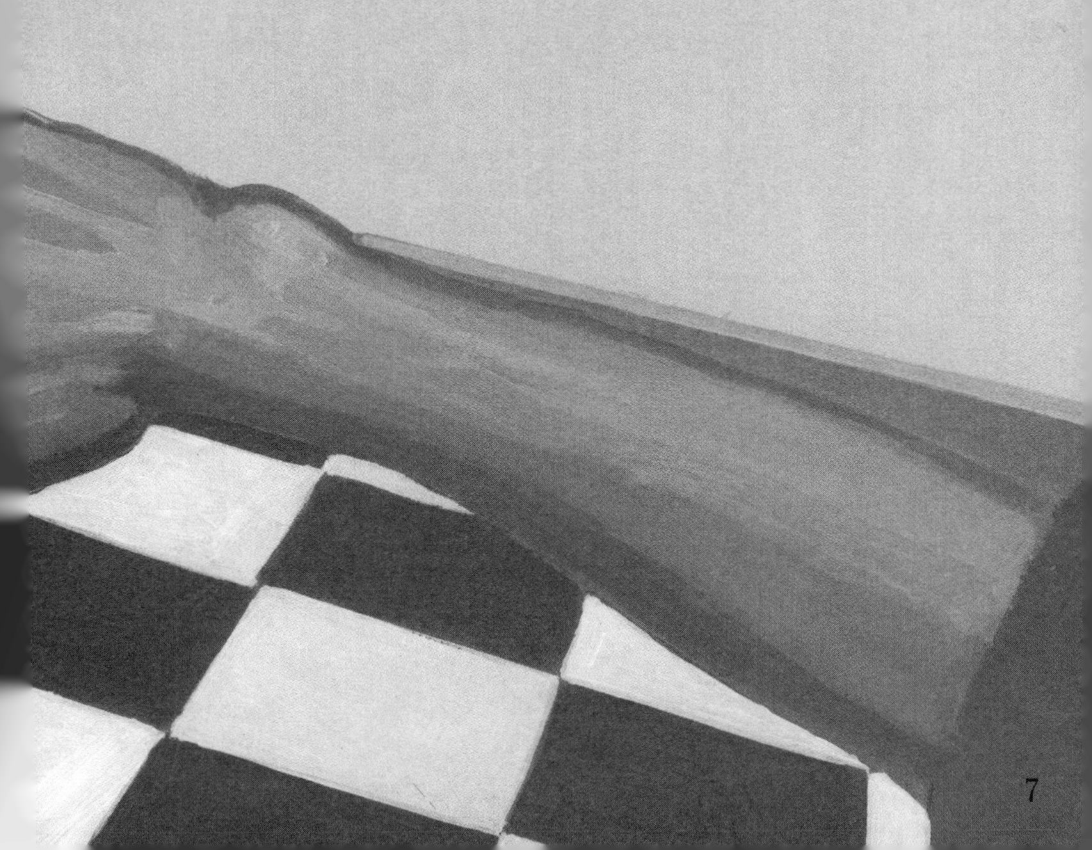

"You getting a cut?" my barber, Alton, asks me.

"Yep, and a shave, too!" I tell him. All the barbers laugh at my joke.

"I've got one in front of you," Alton says.

"Cool," I answer. I head to the arcade game in the back.

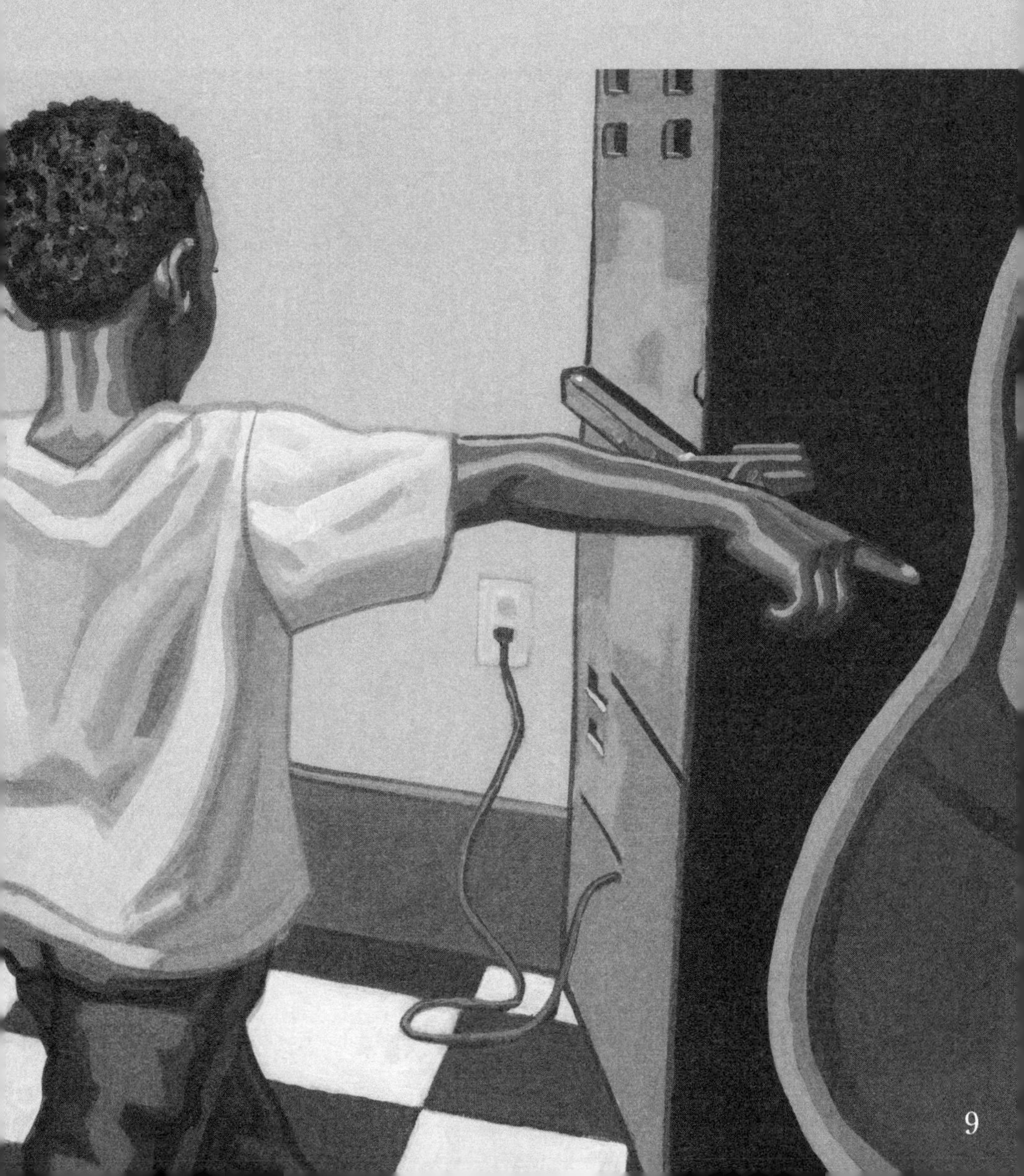

I play three games. Then Alton calls for me. “Yo, Solomon!” he yells as he reaches for the booster seat.

“I’m straight,” I say, sitting down in the big chair. I sit real tall and hold my head high.

Alton smiles and puts the booster seat back under his counter. "What are you getting? A Caesar?"

"No, give me a Fade," I say, "with the sides real close."

Alton snaps a big cape around my shoulders. "So, what you been up to?" Alton always talks with me while he works on my head with his clippers.

"We won our basketball game yesterday!" I say.

"Word! You score?" asks Alton.

"Yeah, four points!" I tell him.

“My man!” he says. “Give me five!” Our hands meet high in the air.

I don’t think it’s such a big deal, but Alton tells the whole shop. Everyone gives me another shout out.

“Go, Big Man!”

“Take ‘em to the hoop!”

I feel real proud of myself.

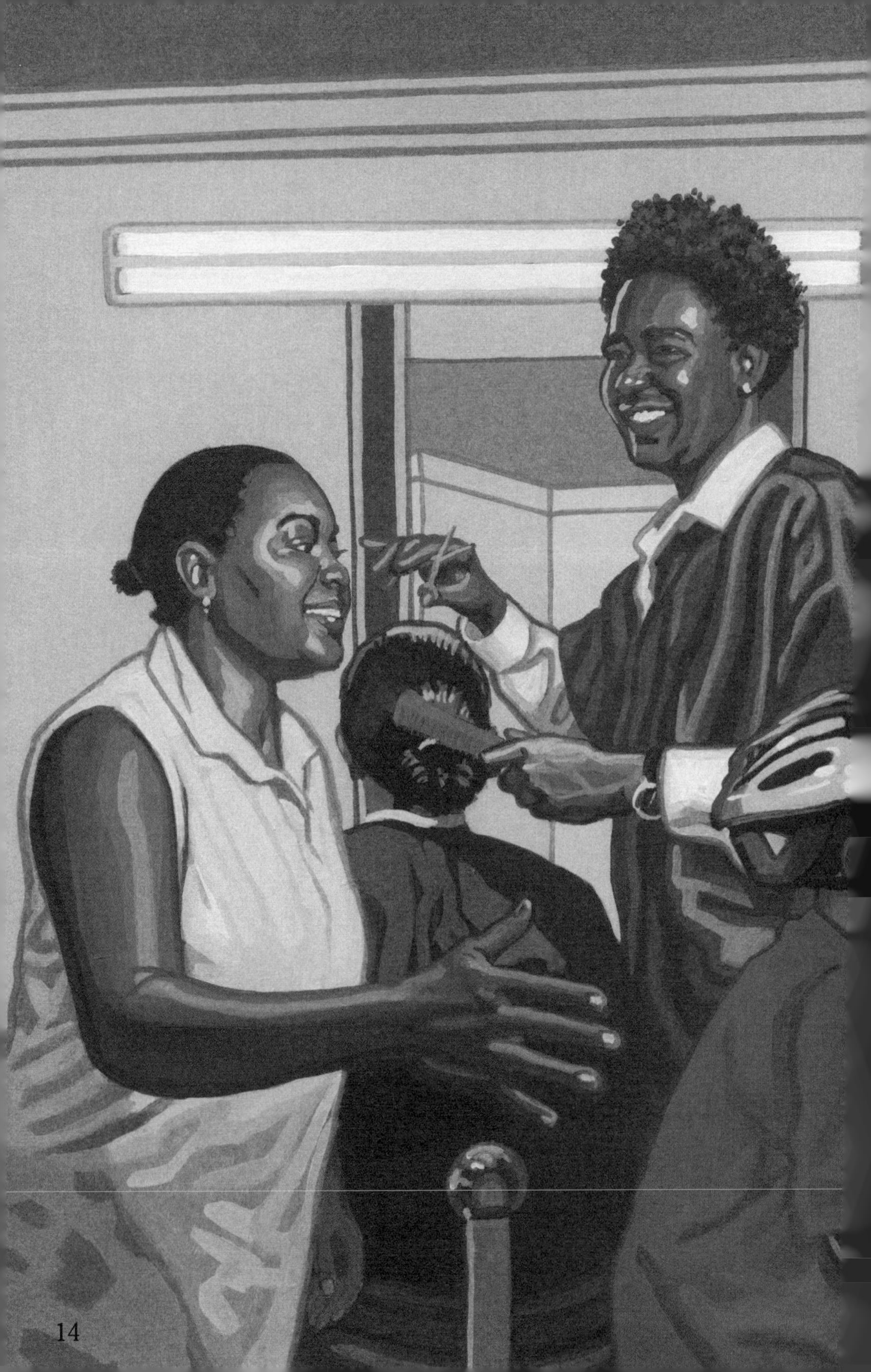

Ding! Ding! The bell above the door sounds off as Mrs. Williams walks in with her son, Jason. "Good morning, everyone," she calls.

"Hello."

"Hi."

"How are you doing?"

All the guys are on their best behavior when a woman comes into The Shop. That shows respect.

"Mark, Jason needs his hair cut. Can I leave him here while I go to the supermarket?"

"Of course, Mrs. Williams," Mark answers.

Then Mrs. Williams looks over at me.

"Well, hello, Solomon!" she says. "Don't you look handsome with that new haircut!"

I look in the mirror. My cut is really shaping up. "Yeah, it's gravy!" I say, patting my head.

Alton taps me gently. He shakes his head "no."

I correct myself. "I mean . . . yes, thank you, Mrs. Williams."

As soon as his mother leaves, Jason bumps fists with all the guys.

“What’s up?” I say when he gets to me.

“Nothing but the sky,” Jason says. He takes a seat to wait for his turn.

"Okay, Superstar, you're done," Alton says as he spins me around. He gives me a hand mirror, so I can see the back of my head in the big mirror.

"You like it?" asks Alton.

"Yeah, it's cool." I check out my sides. They're perfect.

"I think I feel something here," I say. I hold my head back and point to my chin.

Someone laughs loudly. Alton runs the electric razor along the smooth skin of my cheeks and chin anyway. He even splashes on a little aftershave lotion. He sure knows how to please his customers.

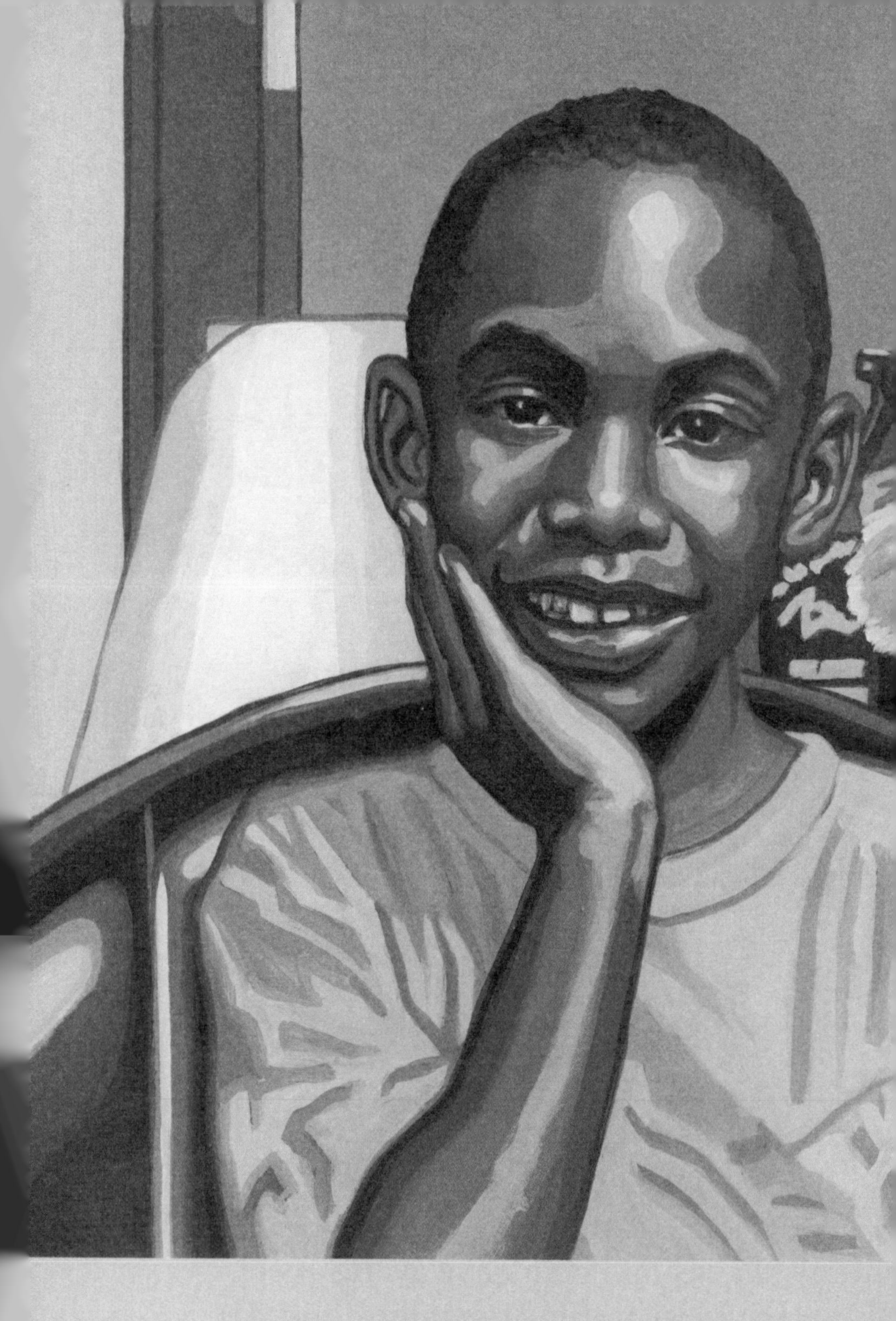

When he's finished, I look in
the mirror and nod my head.

Alton dusts the hair off my neck with a soft brush dipped in powder. The brush tickles, but the powder smells good. Then he takes off my cape.

I reach into my pocket for the money Mom gave me to pay Alton.

"It's on the house," he says, "since you scored in the game yesterday." He means I don't have to pay.

"Thanks, Alton," I say, and I hand him a tip. Mom says you should always tip when you get good service.

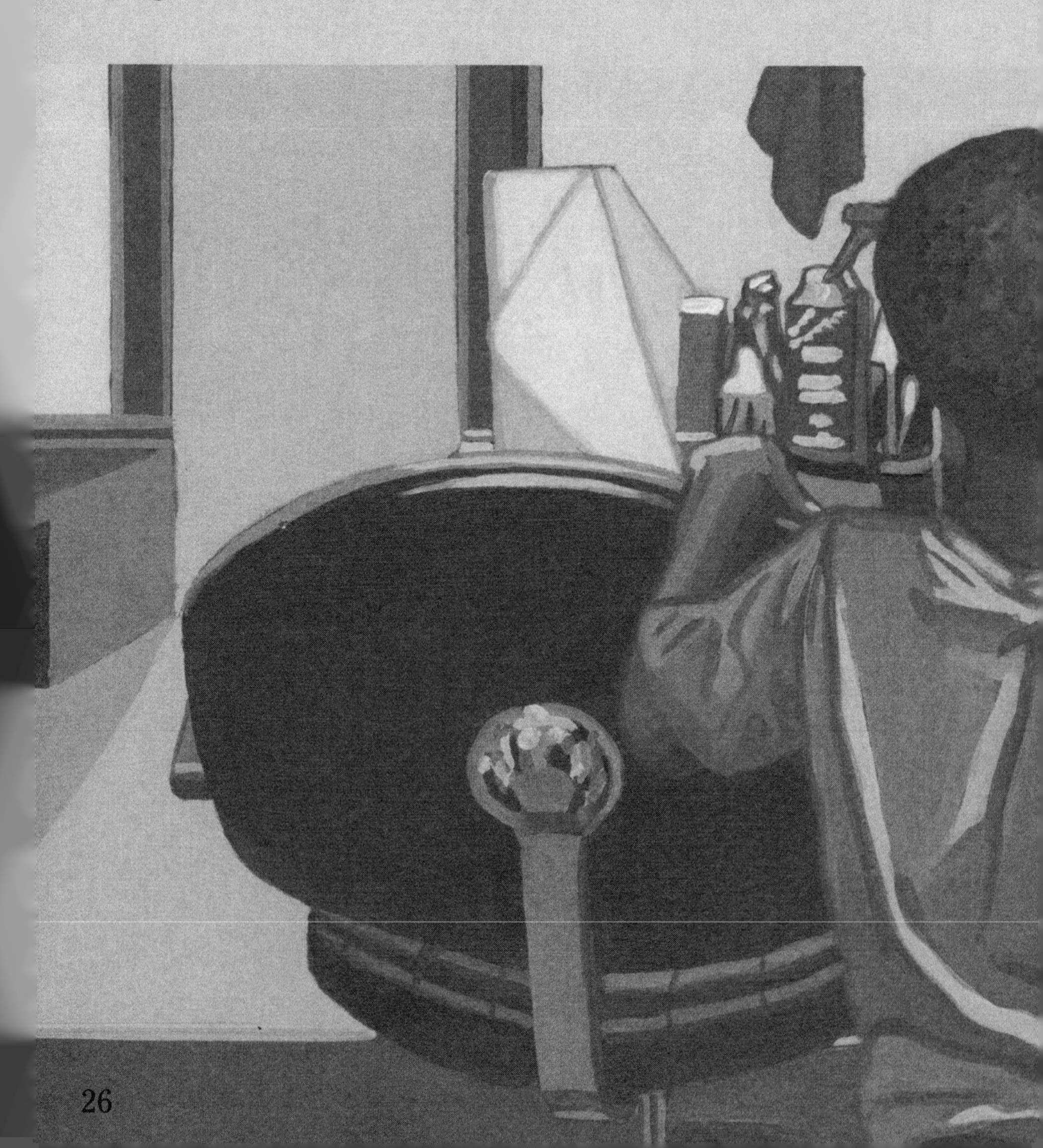

"Catch you later!" Alton says.

"Later," I say, just as Mom walks into The Shop to take me home.

JUST FOR YOU

Here are some fun things for you to do.

It's COOL to Be Nice!

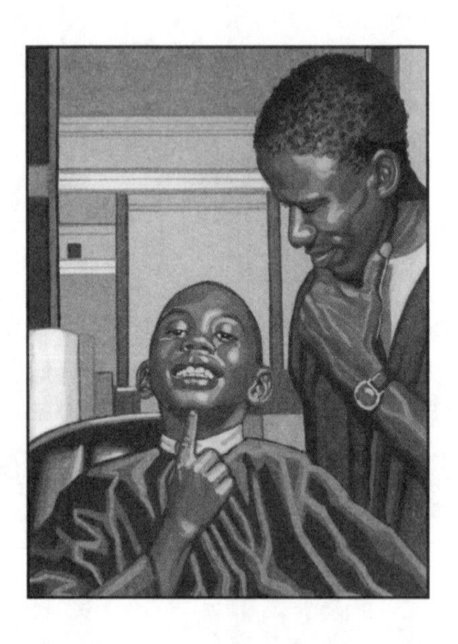

Alton is really nice to Solomon! What does he do and say to make Solomon feel good? ▲

Think of someone YOU know who is very kind. What nice things has that person done for you?

Write a story about the person and why it is cool to be nice. Tell about the kind things he or she does.

Then tell about something nice that YOU want to do for that person!

▲ Some nice things Alton does: He tells everyone about Solomon scoring points in the basketball game; he gives Solomon a pretend shave; he won't let Solomon pay for his haircut.